NEW NORMAL

STUDY GUIDE

JOHN LINDELL

NEW NORMAL

STUDY GUIDE

CHARISMA
HOUSE

Visit the author's website at jamesriver.church and newnormalbook.org.

Library of Congress Cataloging-in-Publication Data:
An application to register this book for cataloging has been submitted to the Library of Congress.
International Standard Book Number: 978-1-62999-940-1
E-book ISBN: 978-1-62999-987-6

21 22 23 24 25 — 987654321
Printed in the United States of America

CONTENTS

Introduction

A NOTE FROM PASTOR JOHN

THE COVER SAYS this is a study guide for my book *New Normal*. It is that, and I don't want this to be a bait and switch here—but I am hoping this will be something more too. While this is a companion piece to the book, my prayer is that it will take you both deeper into the book and deeper into the land God is calling you into. The goal is that this will be not just a study guide but a *field guide* for an undiscovered country you will explore. My hope is that you will not only go deeper into the story of the ancient biblical character of Joshua, around whom much of the book is based, but go deeper into the story of God's delivering work in your own life. I don't want to just go on a journey into the book. I want the Spirit of God to take you on an actual journey of the geography of your soul—a journey where you end up somewhere very different from where you are starting now.

Chances are you have already been on the move. I don't have to be a prophet to tell you that your life looks very different right now than it did not long ago, because the whole world has shifted so much for us all. And many of those changes were not things we would have chosen if it had been up to us.

By nature we are creatures of habit, ordering our lives around routines that give us comfort. We choose the way it's always been, even if the way it's always been is not great—until life *happens* to us in some way. Something happens that we could never have prepared for, often something profoundly difficult.

But with that moment an invitation comes. It is an invitation to come and experience God in a different kind of way, right in the middle of the disruption and chaos that has already dislodged us. And the starting place may simply be that it's no longer feasible to stay where we've been. To intentionally say yes to where God is calling us now opens up the possibility for an entirely different kind of story.

At the time of writing, the COVID-19 pandemic in particular has already marked a global shift in how people think about human connection and intimacy. It has redefined how we travel, how connected our lives are to our neighbors', how fragile our economy is, and how fragile our interconnected ecosystems are. And for a little while many of us couldn't help but muse out loud about how we couldn't wait to get back to the way things were. Yet, as many of us know, whenever we bury a loved one or go through some kind of trauma—a long-term illness, a devastating breakup, depression, a financial collapse—there are some experiences from which there is no going back.

Such is the place we now find ourselves in. There is no going back to "normal." The world we knew before and the way we knew it before simply does not exist. That job, that relationship, that way we had of looking at the world before we lost someone or something close to us—perhaps simply before we lost that naive sense of stability that things would always go on the same way—will never be the same.

What if it's not supposed to? What if "normal," even

when it's not bad, is precisely where most of us get stuck? The land of normal is neither a place of possibility nor a place of battle; it is a place of false comfort based on an illusion that we are more in control than we really are. The land God calls us to is often wilder and will require more of us. It's full of beauty and wonder too—deeper experiences of faith, deeper revelations of God, more deeply connected relationships, and certainly a deeper sense of fulfillment.

The world has changed, and that has dislodged many of us from where we were. Maybe it's felt as if the world has shifted in a way that has broken you down. But could this be the very occasion for God to break you out of where you have been for far too long into the best He has been waiting for you to enter? So consider this your invitation into the new normal God has for you!

HOW TO USE THIS
STUDY GUIDE

Individual study

While I trust that this will be more than just a study guide as you go on this adventure, it is not less than that—so you will need a copy of *New Normal*. As you read the related chapters in the book and then answer the questions, try to stay in a prayerful, open posture, asking God to speak to you and transform you. Keep a Bible handy as well. Since this is intended to be a field guide to exploring new lands in your life and not just for exploring the book, it is intended to be interactive and dynamic, not static. As you read stories from Joshua's life or from my own, always be asking the question "How do these stories interact with my story, and how might my own story play a part in the broader story of what God is doing in the world?"

Bible studies and small groups

If you are a leader, make sure everyone in your group has access to a copy of *New Normal* and this study guide. Each session in this guide corresponds to a chapter or chapters in the book. Ask your members to read the chapters first, then complete the questions in the study guide. Doing both will help them fully participate and grow in grace.

If you are doing this study as a group, whether off-line or online, it is intended to be adapted to the people who show up, however they may gather. The stories of the people who go on this trip with you, the ones they tell and the ones they are living, are part of this journey into new land. Depending on your context, you may want to provide time parameters for how long participants respond to particular questions (perhaps one to two minutes) in order to ensure that all participants have a chance for meaningful engagement and no one feels left out or dominated in the discussion.

Each session contains an opening question to help your group shake off the distractions of the day and focus on the subject matter. A personal word from the author introduces the material, followed by reflection questions. This *New Normal Study Guide* covers the narrative of the life of Joshua, so discussion questions from the Scripture reading are next. Each session closes by challenging the group members to believe for change by integrating these truths into their lives. The final section, "In My Life," is the same for all sessions and gives a moment for the members to hear from God and commit to real change.

Each week, you can lead the group in a discussion using the questions from the week's session. You will probably not have time for all of them, so choose the ones you want to focus on.

Close the study with a creative time of prayer. Cultivating an atmosphere that is prayerful, open, and vulnerable is key for this to be a transformative experience! Remind everyone to prepare for the next week by reading the book and working through the guide.

Encourage your members to take their time as they go through the material. Ask them to consider the questions carefully and approach each one honestly so the Holy Spirit can truly guide them into the particular new land to which they are called.

Session 1
STRENGTH TRAINING

THIS SECTION IS a companion to chapters 1 and 2 of *New Normal*.

FOCUS IN

> What does it mean to be *strong*? What images or people come to your mind when you think of or hear that word? What does strength look like to you?

A PERSONAL WORD

To come into the land God is calling us to, we know deep down it is going to take a level of strength and a depth of trust we have not known before. We wonder if we will be strong enough for what lies ahead. Most of us have had the experience of setting out on some kind of journey—to get physically stronger, to keep a New Year's resolution, to grow or change in some area of our lives—only to find out quickly the challenge was going to be more difficult and more demanding than we anticipated.

Anyone who knows me knows I am competitive. Part of the fun of playing is playing to win, and I am willing to push myself as hard as I have to if I believe victory is on the line. But just like anything else, this competitive drive has its potential pitfalls.

A few years ago I felt as if I was getting a little out of shape and knew I needed a new fitness routine, so I signed up for a class called Bootcamp. The name says it all. It was an hour of nonstop intensive cardio, made up of a seemingly unending onslaught of bear crawls, floor sweepers, mountain climbers, push-ups, sit-ups, squat jumps, and anything else my instructor (a.k.a. the drill sergeant) could dream up.

I showed up on the first day to find the gym full of mostly twenty- and thirty-year-olds. At this point I should mention I was turning fifty that year! Undeterred, I decided to prove to myself and everyone else who might be watching that I could win. Unfortunately my long-dormant muscles hadn't gotten the memo! It would be a while before my body could match my competitive drive. After that first session, I felt fine when I left the gym. It wasn't until the next day when I went to get out of bed that my legs, which had pumped so hard the morning before, were too stiff and sore to navigate any incline. Forget climbing stairs; that wasn't happening. My desire to compete had backfired. And it was obvious that growing stronger would take time and training.

That's benign enough, but we know that beyond aspiring to get physically stronger, any real change in our lives requires more than just another New Year's resolution. All of us face spiritual resistance to stepping into the land that God is calling us into—because the stakes are considerably higher. That's why all of Scripture frames the spiritual growth that results in a physically different life as a battle with ourselves and with spiritual forces of evil. When we get serious about growing in our faith, going deeper in our connection with God, and finding the land God has called us to explore, the resistance will be real, intense, and fierce. No matter how good our intentions are, even the best of us will hit a wall or a challenge that will test our resolve and make us question whether we had any business setting out on this journey in the first place. And no matter how much (or little) you've been to the gym, you will find out very quickly that physical strength simply will not be enough.

REFLECTION

> ➤ Have you ever had a time in your life when you tried to make some kind of meaningful change or go on some kind of new journey, only to quickly face real resistance and hit a wall? What did that look like for you?

> ➤ As we set out on this journey of faith, what do you think "the land" might be that God is calling you to enter—that would require deeper faith and a deeper trust and reliance

on God's strength than you've ever known before?

➤ When we set out on such a faith journey, it often starts with circumstances shifting in our lives that force our hand—it is simply no longer an option to stay where we are. For Joshua, it was surely the painful experience of the death of Moses that turned out to be the beginning of a whole new adventure with God. Can you think of a time in your life when a door closed in a way that was sad or scary at the time but opened up space for God to do something new? Can you think of a way that might be happening in your life right now?

Tucked within the Old Testament story of Joshua, we see that the strength a new normal requires is not defined within the typical boundaries of how we seek strength. Not only does God tell Joshua repeatedly not to be afraid, but God also tells him over and over to "be strong and courageous, for you shall cause this people to inherit the land that I swore to their fathers" (Josh. 1:6). That's perhaps easier said than done, especially in a world where strength is so ambiguously defined. What exactly does it mean to be strong or to act strong? Is being brave synonymous with big muscles, rigid determination, or utter fearlessness?

On the contrary, we often have our most primal encounter with fear just as God calls us into the new normal. Feeling the fear doesn't necessarily mean you are in the wrong place at the wrong time. It often means you are on the precipice of the new land God is calling you to enter.

> What would make you afraid to go on this journey—what scares you about attempting to enter "the land"? What has held you back before, and what is holding you back now?

> Is it possible to choose to be strong and courageous and yet still feel scared sometimes? Is faith a feeling? Or is it possible to move forward in faith, no matter what feelings may come and go?

> When you hear the words "Do not be afraid," are they words of comfort or words of rebuke? Do you hear them as the words of loving encouragement from a parent who wants you to feel safe—or from an irritated authoritarian who is really saying, "You are dumb to be afraid"?

> How different would your life be if you really, honestly believed you had no reasons to be afraid?

> We all have our own battles to fight to come into "the land." How do you hope this study will help you in yours? What changes do you hope to make in your relationship with God or with others? In your own spiritual geography, where would you hope to be when this study is over?

FROM THE BIBLE

Chapter 2 highlights one of the ways we can build our faith and the faith of those around us: the practice of speaking with courage. Standing on the banks of the Jordan River, the people of God needed to hear words of courage. They needed someone who would dare to speak the courage and hope of God over them and into them. Joshua was up for the challenge:

> Joshua said to the people of Israel, "Come here and listen to the words of the LORD your God.... Here is how you shall know that the living God is among you and that he will without fail drive out from before you the Canaanites, the Hittites, the Hivites, the Perizzites, the Girgashites, the Amorites, and the Jebusites."
>
> —JOSHUA 3:9–10

Hearing these words of encouragement made all the difference for these early Hebrews, and words of encouragement will make all the difference for us. We all need a faithful community to speak God's Word over us and into us, to see God's hand and calling on us when we cannot see it for ourselves. The story of a person's entire life can take on a different trajectory because one person chooses to speak with spiritual courage in their conversations!

> ‣ If you are doing the study as an individual, take a few moments to prayerfully reflect

on some people in your life who could benefit from these kinds of encouraging words—words of courage, strength, reminders to not be afraid. "I believe in you," "I am praying for you," "I see God's goodness and kindness in you," or "You are going to make it" are powerful words to hear. Consider making a list of the first three names that come to your mind, and contact them in some form this week to share whatever life-giving words you feel would serve them best.

> If you are doing the study as a group, you have already had the opportunity to share some vulnerable things about the invitation to change in your own life and some of the fears that have held you back. This is an opportunity to share this important practice with your group. Go around the room and take a few moments to intentionally share words of encouragement with one another, based on what needs/desires have been shared so far. Having deep knowledge of everyone around you is not required—responding to the needs that have been articulated so far, even from people you don't know well, is welcome. The

ground rule is this is not a time for correction, or really even advice—just encouragement, to speak words of life, comfort, and hope. After everyone who feels comfortable sharing has had an opportunity to do so, this could be a perfect opportunity to incorporate a time of praying over one another.

BELIEVE FOR CHANGE

> If you are going to be strong and unafraid, you have to begin to trust what God says to you and what God says about you—which is generally so much better than what we say to ourselves, about ourselves! Here are a few encouraging statements that are hard to believe when we've been living from a place of fear. Take a few moments to read through them slowly and reflectively, asking God to show you if any of these particular phrases are for you to receive right now. Pay attention to what you feel when you read each phrase, what these words might break open in you, and even what you might be resistant to, which could be equally important:

» God is never going to give up on you.

» Your life is not an accident, and you are not a disappointment.

» God is going to finish the good work He has started in you.

» You have never, ever, ever been alone—even in your worst moments—and you aren't alone right now.

» There is more than enough for you.

» Your past does not define you.

» God delights in who you are and how you are made.

> Which of these statements were difficult for you to accept? Why?

IN MY LIFE

> What stands out for you from the study this week?

> What adjustments will you make in your life because of what you've learned?

➤ How will your relationship with God and
   your relationships with others change?

Session 2

SETTING YOURSELF UP FOR A MIRACLE

THIS SESSION IS a companion to chapters 3 and 4 of *New Normal*.

FOCUS IN

> Have you ever witnessed—or experienced— a miracle? Do you believe that miracles still happen today?

A PERSONAL WORD

This session is about two things: remembering what God has done for us in the past and making space for what God wants to do for us in the present and future. We remember what God has done for us before—not because God is necessarily going to deliver us the same way again the next time but to remind ourselves that God is always our Deliverer!

We also make space for what God wants to do in us now. *Consecration* is a beautiful word for that act of setting aside time and space to make room for the activity of God's Spirit in our lives. Consecration is not about effort; it's about attention. It's about making space for God. Consecration means setting ourselves apart for an intended purpose. At times throughout history, buildings and objects have been set apart for sacred use. The temple and the ark of the covenant were the places where God's presence dwelled in sacred space. Entering those places required consecration.

It has become significant, both in my life and in the life of James River Church, to have established seasons of prayer and fasting, precisely because these are times of consecration. Among Christian spiritual practices, fasting can be especially misunderstood because it can be construed as attempting to prove our devotion to God with the force of sheer human effort. Nothing could be further from the truth! We fast because sometimes our capacity to hear God gets cluttered and we want to remove all the debris that could keep us from hearing and seeing clearly. Fasting is a way of hitting our inner spiritual reset button. It's not unlike when you lose your internet connection and you have to unplug the router and plug it back in. The signal doesn't ever change—God is always speaking! But our capacity to hear and see does get overwhelmed. So sometimes we have to find ways to reset our inner router.

A couple of years ago a friend named Tom got some very bad news. It's the kind of diagnosis that no one wants to hear. His doctor told him that he had stage III lymphoma with a 10 percent chance of survival, even if he had surgery. You would think that news would be devastating to Tom and his family. There was a 90 percent chance his life was over! The doctor advised that it was time to say his goodbyes, plan the funeral, and make sure his affairs were in order. So

Tom and his family started to plan, but their planning was different from what most people expected. He began to plan for a miracle.

He knew he needed people to pray, so he took every opportunity to ask people to do exactly that. At James River Church we encourage people to write down what they are asking God to do on a prayer card so that others in the church can pray with them. And that's what Tom did—thirty-four times!

As Tom neared the date of his operation, he felt compelled to make sure that he and his family seized the opportunity God was giving them to interact with the specific people they were going to encounter during his hospital stay. He knew this was likely the only time he would ever see or interact with these nurses, doctors, and hospital staff members who would be part of his care. So Tom wanted to do something that he believed God could specifically speak through to every single person he saw.

With that in mind, he and his wife went through their Bibles and identified certain verses they believed God would use to encourage particular people. They chose verses such as Job 42:1–2: "Job answered GOD: 'I'm convinced: You can do anything and everything. Nothing and no one can upset your plans'" (MSG). Then Tom and his family printed out the verses and attached each verse to a piece of candy.

On the day I visited him in the hospital in advance of his surgery, I anticipated a solemn environment with a family that would likely be emotional in the face of such a dire situation. What I walked into was almost the complete opposite of what I had expected. The room was a party, and Tom was the host! There was music playing and candy being passed out, and the family was filled with joyful confidence about what God was going to do! Their words were not filled with the grim dread of what the future might hold but with the ways that God's power might invade their hospital stay and work in Tom's body and how the Lord might speak to the medical team caring for him. Tom wasn't unaware of the severity of the circumstances or in denial of the diagnosis, but he also wasn't willing to deny the power of God. And sure enough, after the surgery Tom was completely, miraculously declared cancer-free.

To some people I'm sure Tom's family may have looked a little crazy, praying and speaking words of faith when he was virtually given a medical death sentence. But this is precisely why consecration is so crucial—entering the new land of God's best requires our going places we have not been to before and learning to follow the presence of God wherever it leads us, even when it doesn't make sense to us or the people around us.

We have seen many miracles come out of our times of consecration at James River. God's direction and provision have always followed those times of quiet consecration.

REFLECTION

> Have you ever fasted before? Was it a positive or negative experience? What did you learn from it?

> What are some other ways you think people can consecrate themselves in the life they live for God?

Keep in mind that miracles cannot be earned by good behavior! But they can be anticipated by our faith. Everybody wants to see miracles, but not everyone makes space for them. Of course, you cannot manufacture a miracle. Miracles are part of God's job description, not yours. You can't make the moment happen; you can't force anything. And because God the Father loves to give His children good gifts, you don't have to beg, plead, work anything up, or work everything out. You are not responsible for the miracle-making. But what you can and *must* do is make space for the miracle—you can make yourself ready.

You can clear room for God to do what only God can do. That's what consecration is all about.

> What is the difference between making space for God to move and trying to earn God's approval, or force God's hand with some kind of you-scratch-my-back-I-scratch-yours quid pro quo thing? How is consecration different from trying to earn God's acceptance or even trying to earn a miracle?

> Is there a particular miracle you are longing for in your life right now? Do you believe God can—or would—do it? Or does it feel risky to admit that longing out loud, for fear that you might be disappointed?

> What could you fast—what could you give up or set aside—to create space to hear the voice of God in your life more clearly? Remember, this is not about punishment; it is about making space. How long could your fast be? How could you use the time, energy, and effort that would

normally go into that thing you are temporarily laying down to lean more intentionally into your relationship with God? Here is a list of a few ideas of things you could fast/ways you could fast/ways to consecrate yourself:

» Fast from food one to two days a week for a season or for an entire week or for designated meals.

» Set aside a certain amount of additional time each morning for prayer and meditation on God's Word.

» Or create your own idea for a time of fasting or consecration right here:

> After taking a few moments to prayerfully contemplate how you might be called to be intentional about consecrating yourself, write out your plan for this set-aside time. (If you are doing the study as a group, you may want to consider or discuss a group act or time of consecration that you share together.)

FROM THE BIBLE

Just before the Israelites followed Joshua into the land they had longed for, there was a crucial pause: "Then Joshua said to the people, 'Consecrate yourselves, for tomorrow the LORD will do wonders among you'" (Josh. 3:5). So much of our lives is about deadlines and demanding schedules to make the most of each day. But consecration always requires waiting. We have to take time to wait on God. Before we move into the land of blessing, there have to be moments for watching, looking, and seeing. The people of God "camped" before they "crossed over." They had three days to sit, to consider the impossibility of crossing a flooded river, to dream about the wonders God would work, and to draw closer to God.

In this particular text, they were watching a flood. Day by day they saw objects floating down the river in front of them—probably big trees and other debris. The Jordan River is not that big, but the Israelites had camped on its banks in the rainy season with the snow melting off Mount Hermon and the water coming down into the Sea of Galilee. If you visit Israel today, the spring runoff has been tamed, and the Jordan rarely surges. But in Joshua's day the Jordan River would be a swollen, rushing, angry river of debris. The people knew a crossing needed to take place, but they were acutely aware that it was humanly impossible! Coming into the new land God has for you often means taking a long and sober look at what lies ahead. Faith is not denial, not a way of simply burying your head in the sand. Faith is radically honest about what is in front of us.

For Joshua, the directions that came then were, by human standards, bizarre and disorienting. The people of God had spent three days looking at the overflowing river. Now they were given orders to go to a place they had not been to and to a path that would take them through that flooding river. They were charged to follow the ark of the covenant as it headed right toward a flooded river. It didn't make any sense. You can't cross a flooded river! You can't—unless God performs a miracle. You can't cross a flooded river unless God does what only He can do to take you into a new normal.

He sent the priests ahead, carrying the ark of the covenant. This act was not empty or ceremonial. The ark represented the presence of God going before them, and if God did not go before them, they had no chance. He watched the priests' feet descend into the mud as they got closer to the water, but their pace was slow, deliberate, and steady. They had prepared themselves for this; they had made their hearts ready, and their bodies followed suit.

God had given Joshua a very particular command for the priests carrying the ark: "When you come to the brink of the waters of the Jordan, you shall stand still in the Jordan" (3:8). As the priests walked in sync with one another, as measured as a bride walking down the aisle, their feet slowly dipped in the edge, feeling the cool, refreshing water between their toes.

They had taken steps of faith, and there was nothing left for them to do. Whatever happened or did not happen now, it was not up to them. Coming into the flooded waters during harvest season, they stopped and simply stood there.

When the Israelites stopped striving and just stood still, the impossible happened. The waters flowing from above stood still and rose in a single heap on one side. The priests stood still on the now bone-dry ground in the middle of the Jordan River while the entire nation crossed to the other side.

Just as it happened to them, it will happen for you. Prepare your heart and sanctify your mind. But when it is time to walk through the river, stand still— even though people will tell you that you are crazy for just standing there, even though you may fear looking silly or the stray thought comes: "But what if *nothing* happens?" The miracle comes not for the strongest, the fastest, or those with the most will-power; the miracle comes to those who *stop, stand still, and wait.* It comes to those who are looking.

> ➤ The Israelites had waited through forty years of wilderness, wandering, all the while dreaming of the Promised Land. By that point they were surely ready to get on with it! And yet there was this specific instruction to pause and take the time to consecrate themselves, "for tomorrow the LORD will do wonders among you." Why do you think they

NEW NORMAL STUDY GUIDE

needed this intentional, set-aside time—after
waiting so long already?

> Have you ever had a time in your life when
  you felt as if God was directing you to do
  something to make room for Him as an act of
  consecration, that may have seemed strange
  at the time to everybody else?

> Why is it important to take time to assess the
  journey that is ahead realistically—to "count
  the cost," in Jesus' phrase? How is moving
  forward in faith different from just living in
  denial of the reality of the challenges/obsta-
  cles ahead?

> We looked at how consecration is a way of
  paying attention, of looking for God to move.
  Do you think it is possible that God is moving

on behalf of some people in powerful ways but they fail to recognize it simply because they are not consecrating themselves—because they are not paying attention?

BELIEVE FOR CHANGE

One of the ways we prepare for what God wants to do in us in the present and in the future is by reminding ourselves of the faithfulness of God in the past. Joshua 4:21–22 says, "In the future when your descendants ask their parents, 'What do these stones mean?' tell them, 'Israel crossed the Jordan on dry ground'" (NIV). God anticipated these conversations would happen in families. He told them that their children would ask them what the stones mean. Families can build altars to what God has done. Single people can build altars to the faithfulness of God. Friends can come up with ways to remember the goodness of God together. The important thing is that we do something concrete to remind us, something to remember.

> Have you ever built an altar? When is a time in your life when God did something worth building an altar for?

NEW NORMAL STUDY GUIDE

> What is something you could do now to remember what God did in a way that keeps the faithfulness of God constantly in front of you in the days ahead? Gathering stones still works, but you can use anything. You can do this practice on your own, but this activity, in particular, is especially powerful when done with a group. Even if it's just a few friends or family members, it helps when everyone can remind one another what God has done in us. Take a few moments to reflect prayerfully and remember something good God has done for you. Write down an idea or two of how you might creatively build an altar to commemorate that experience.

IN MY LIFE

> What stands out for you from the study this week?

➤ What adjustments will you make in your life because of what you've learned?

➤ How will your relationship with God and your relationships with others change?

Session 3
LETTING GO

T

HIS SESSION IS a companion to chapter 5 of *New Normal.*

FOCUS IN

> Have you ever had a time in your life when you really wanted to move forward in some new direction—but had to let go of someone or something painful before you were able to go any further?

A PERSONAL WORD

There is a familiar pattern to change: God nudges us toward the new normal, but upon our arrival we can feel that something is missing. We are excited about the land, but we can find ourselves wondering if we have all we need.

In reality, in the early stages of coming into the new normal, we rarely need to *add* anything, but there is almost always something we hold on to that we need to *subtract.* The routine of life can numb us to the need for change. Besides, familiarity brings with it a comfort like a favorite pair of shoes. We would like a new normal; we just aren't ready until we let go of a few things.

The internal monologue looks like this: Somewhere

deep down, you know that the relationship isn't right. But the idea of severing it would be too painful or cause too much chaos in the short term, so you put off the conversation and delay the change, hoping things will somehow work out for the best.

For some, relaxation seems impossible without the buzz of another drink, so you tell yourself that maybe when work is less stressful, the habit of drinking to unwind will change. Or maybe you know deep down that God is nudging you to do something else with your life vocationally. Still, it would hurt too much to sacrifice the extra income right now, so you will wait until you know there is absolute financial security on the other side of doing what you believe God is calling you to do. Or you'll try to deal with what you know has become an addiction to pornography when your sexual relationship with your spouse feels easier and more fulfilling.

Spoiler alert: There is never a convenient time to do the one nagging thing God has been prompting you to do. It will never be easy. That's why you've put it off for a thousand Mondays. There will never be a time when things are stable enough, steady enough, or calm enough that deciding to cut off an unnecessary attachment is something you feel like doing. Sometimes you just get sick and tired of being sick and tired, and sometimes the voice of God gets louder and louder until you deal with it. Other times, the fear that you'll never hear His voice again unless you change prompts the necessary actions. We have to get to a place where, circumstantially, the old way of life just doesn't work for us anymore and we finally decide we've had enough. We can repeat the same old patterns that have held us back on an endless loop, or we can make a painful cut.

Here's the catch: the provision rarely comes first. Often we are presented with the opportunity to sever something that feels vital to us, not knowing whether God will provide on the other side.

I'm reminded of my friend Joel, who felt for years that God was calling him to vocational ministry. He and his young wife would have dreams about it every week. They felt certain they were supposed to take a ministry position that paid twenty-five dollars a week. But he had a lucrative job, and taking the leap felt ridiculous. Finally, worn down by the constant sense that he wasn't in the right vocation, he gave his two weeks' notice, left his job, and took the ministry position. Within weeks of accepting the role, mysterious checks started coming in whenever the bills were due. He once had a stranger flag him down on the interstate in rural Indiana—he assumed the stranger needed some kind of roadside help with his car—only to tell him that God spoke to him and told him to give him the $250 he had in his wallet. But none of that would have happened unless and until he had made the cut.

I've seen it happen in unhealthy dating relationships—people staying in something they know is not God's best with the logic that it's not ideal, but it's

OK. "I'll make do until God sends something better along." But that's not how it works.

God rarely sends what you need while you are hanging on to something you know you don't need. If you have an unhealthy habit in your life that you think you can't live without, you can't wait until something better comes along to fill the void—you have to sever the cord first and trust that God will provide on the other side. There's no getting around the risk involved—you don't get to half cut and then wait and see. This cutting away is the hardest step of obedience, but it cannot be skipped.

REFLECTION

> What's the most painful thing you've ever had to let go of?

> Why do you think it is that God often doesn't send the provision we need until we let go of the thing we really don't need anymore?

> Why is it always so hard to let go?

Before the Israelites would be able to enter the land of blessing and keep living in a new normal, they would need to address an area of delayed obedience. In this place, what was important to God would have to become most important to them— the place of reordering their priorities to align with God's priorities.

> If you are going to move into the new normal, this is a crucial question: Is there something God has asked you to do that you have left undone? Is there something that you know God has wanted you to deal with, but you haven't responded to what was spoken to your heart? It could be a besetting sin—an addiction, a habit, or something you call a hobby that, in truth, has more of a hold on you than you do on it. It could be a relationship that has not been reconciled, where you know you are being led to go back, make an apology, and make amends. Take a few moments to prayerfully reflect on these questions and write down whatever you feel stirring in response.

FROM THE BIBLE

Read Joshua 5:2–9, the story of the Israelites being circumcised again. Especially note verses 8–9 (NIV):

> And after the whole nation had been circumcised, they remained where they were in camp until they were healed. Then the LORD said to Joshua, "Today I have rolled away the reproach of Egypt from you." So the place has been called Gilgal to this day.

After forty years of wandering in the wilderness, the people of God finally crossed over into the land. The relief in the air was palpable; they could finally feel their feet touch the ground of that fabled land where the milk and honey flowed, where the grass and dirt beneath them felt charged with the promise of God. He had pledged this territory to their ancestors, and now they were finally stepping into it, getting their first taste of the new normal. They knew there would still be battles to fight, but the ground was lush and the future bright. It felt like the good life.

But as they camped at the place called Gilgal, the past caught up with them. God had commanded their ancestors that every male be circumcised, and yet none of the men of Joshua's generation had obeyed this command.

Circumcision involves the cutting away of the flesh from the tip of the male reproductive organ. God

NEW NORMAL STUDY GUIDE

commanded that the circumcision be performed on the eighth day after the child's birth. Think of how much easier it would have been to follow God's original command! It's a fact: delayed obedience often complicates our lives and can result in painful circumstances our obedience would have avoided.

To the modern mindset, a Scripture passage like Joshua chapter 5 might seem like an exercise in divine arbitrariness. What merit could there possibly be in a divine being telling a group of grown men on the heels of crossing into the land of their dreams to stop marching so every male could cut the foreskin off his genitals? It's one thing as a procedure for a baby but a crippling, wrenching experience for grown men who are ostensibly being prepared for battle just around the corner.

As we saw in a previous chapter, God told the people to follow the ark of the covenant right toward the flooding river. God seems to use counterintuitive measures to teach us to trust divine initiatives over our most basic human instincts. But I don't think His choice is arbitrary at all. In Joshua 5:9 God says, "Today I have rolled away the reproach of Egypt from you." That's why to this day that location is called Gilgal, which means "a rolling away."[1] Gilgal, the place where God dealt with Israel's long-delayed obedience, is also the place where God dealt with His people's *shame*.

We know more and more now about how shame affects us, not only psychologically but physically.

Shame produces hiding, and secrets kill us. The work of popular authors such as Ed Welch has brought the topic of shame into our public discourse. We are just beginning to understand how shame can affect the body and even be stored in the body through multiple generations. Our bodies do not forget things.

At Gilgal, God forced His people to confront their past and bring the truth of their disobedience into the light. Without this bold and courageous act, this generation would be condemned to repeat the same mistakes. In a very public act of obedience, the people of God were breaking the cycle of disobedience and shame. They were resetting the entire story. Yes, there would be pain involved in this cutting away. But note that Gilgal was not named as the place of pain but the place where their shame was rolled away!

But there is something else too. Gilgal is not just the place for the cutting away—Gilgal is also a place of *healing*. After this cutting away, God isn't asking the people to charge ahead to the next fight—that's how a lot of us got ourselves in this kind of shape to begin with. We charged from one battle to the next without paying attention to unhealed wounds, unhealed trauma, and unhealthy patterns.

When you are in Gilgal and you are cutting away the thing, or the relationship, or the substance you thought you needed so desperately, it might feel as if you aren't going to make it. But take heart. Gilgal is not the place where you die; it's the place where your *reproach* dies, where your *shame* dies. It's the place where the last remnants of the old life, the unhealthy you, are cut away so you can fully inhabit this new land and journey into your new normal.

BELIEVE FOR CHANGE

> It could also be said that Gilgal is a place of separation. Sometimes the thing you need to be separated from, the thing you need to sever, is not external but internal. Some of the things you have attached to are not things God can bless, and they have no place in the land God is calling you into now. Gilgal is a place of letting go of things you don't need. They are things you weren't meant to carry with you anyway. Here is a list of things you might need to separate from. Read these slowly and prayerfully, and note at which of these phrases you feel deep resonance—or even just deep resistance, which is equally telling:

  » Shame about your past

  » Insecurity

  » An attitude of pride or self-indulgence

  » An addiction to a substance or to technology

  » A lingering racial prejudice

» A slight or resentment you have hidden away deep inside and harbored for years

» Legalism

» A relationship that is toxic or where you are hanging on too tightly

» Hurtful words/labels that have been spoken over you in the past

» The need to be in control

> After spending a few minutes prayerfully considering this list, what is that thing you know in your belly you need to cut away? I hate to tell you, but whatever you are afraid it might be is probably what it is. You know it precisely because you feel yourself hanging on too tightly—that's why you are so afraid to let go. It is scary to let go of something so attached, something you think you need. It is the most radical and frightening act of trust. It is also the ultimate key to freedom in the land, the most powerful act of release into the new normal.

> Whatever or whoever it is, why don't you just go ahead and name it right now and hand it over to the One who knows you best and loves you most? And precisely because it is such a big deal for you to relinquish control and let go, why don't you write a short prayer officially telling God that He can have it? It can take whatever form you want but should be some version of saying, "God, I hear Your voice, and I am letting go of _____ to You." Sit with this for a few minutes. It's OK to take your time. It's OK to tell God you're scared to let go, even while you are telling God you are letting go. It's OK to shed some tears. Remember, Gilgal is a place of separation—but it is also a place of healing!

IN MY LIFE

> What stands out for you from the study this week?

➤ What adjustments will you make in your life
because of what you've learned?

➤ How will your relationship with God and
your relationships with others change?

Session 4

SEEING WHAT GOD SEES

THIS SESSION IS a companion to chapter 6 of *New Normal.*

FOCUS IN

> Have you ever had a moment in your life when the unseen world, or spiritual realm, seemed to break into the human realm of what we can see? Maybe for just a moment you *knew something of how much you don't know* about the spiritual realm or were able to *see something of how much you don't see*? How did you come to that kind of seeing, and how did it change your perspective?

A PERSONAL WORD

The unseen realities of life are the greater realities. But most of the time, we only evaluate what's in front of us based on what we can see with our physical eyes. In other words, we only see what we can see— and most of the time, we see the world from a natural point of view rather than a spiritual one. When we are coming into the land God has for us, the task is to learn to see the world and our lives as God sees them. Sometimes that happens best when life seems to come entirely off the rails from our limited human perspective.

It wasn't that long ago that I hit a season when my life seemed to change overnight. I had been in Rome leading a tour on the journeys of the apostle Paul. Thankfully, Paul wrote a lot about weakness, because that was all I felt when I went from leading a tour to lying flat on my back on a gurney with a blood clot in my brain. As beautiful as Italy is, all I could think about was getting myself back home to the world I knew.

Once we got back to the States, I still wasn't well, so we headed to Colorado, sure that some days in the mountains would bring the healing and rest I needed. On our third day in Vail, I talked Debbie and my daughter, Savannah, into renting some electric bikes. It was a gorgeous day as we rode along a mountain stream. As we stopped to take some pictures, Debbie's foot became caught in the bike, and she fell, shattering her pelvis. Her recovery would require fourteen days in the hospital. Needless to say, it was a difficult time for both of us.

As time passed, instead of me getting stronger, my weight continued to drop until I became visibly gaunt. Debbie grew more worried about my health and wondered what was happening. The board of the church wanted to send me to Mayo Clinic, so finally I went. Ultimately they diagnosed me with an autonomic condition that involved excruciating fatigue. Worse yet, there was no cure.

Every year during the summer, our church participates in twenty-one days of prayer and fasting. While on the fast that following year, I let the church people know the severity of my situation and asked them to pray for me. I don't know what I expected to feel as they prayed for me, but what I felt most was a deep sense of their love for me. And in the days that followed, it became obvious that God had touched my heart physically. Instead of repeated bouts where my heart rate rose to over two hundred beats per minute, it was now calm.

Still, the fatigue was relentless and hadn't diminished. Amid this situation I kept pressing forward on Sunday mornings to preach at the church as best I could. One Sunday morning about five weeks after that initial touch from God, a couple from the church felt led to anoint me with oil and pray for me. When they did, I felt the fiery presence of the Lord from my head to my feet. Something definitive happened. As I returned to my seat, I turned to Debbie and said, "God just healed me." At the core of my being, I knew God had touched me. Over the next six months, I gained forty pounds, and my strength returned.

What does all that have to do with you? When everything looks as if it's over from your point of view, and you feel as if you have come to a dead end, God calls you to another way of seeing. In God's way of seeing the world, there are no dead ends. What looks like the end to you may only be the beginning of a whole new chapter in this story of God's faithfulness that is being written with your very life. A miracle is not a fluke or a one-time exception. Whenever you see impossibility, God wants to give you eyes to see what is only possible by His great power at work in your life.

This is what it means to follow the God of Joshua, who took His people from the wilderness to the land where milk and honey flowed. God was always on the move then. God is still on the move now.

REFLECTION

> What difference do you think it makes in your life to see things from God's perspective, as opposed to just a human perspective?

> Can you think of a time in your life when you were convinced that there was no solution and no way out from a human point of view but God had a completely different perspective on your situation?

> If you had to summarize it in a single sentence, what do you think is the primary difference between how humans see and how God sees? Another way of putting it: What does God see that we don't?

Our ability to see through the eyes of faith determines the entire trajectory of our lives. According to Proverbs 29:18, "If people can't see what God is doing, they stumble all over themselves" (MSG). A conqueror doesn't need to be the strongest, fastest, or smartest. In everything that matters, all we need to be able to win is the ability to *see.* More than anything else, having the vision to see what God sees in any given battle determines whether we will win that battle.

The question is not whether God is doing something. God is always doing something! The question is, *What* is God doing? We need a vision of a deeper reality than what is immediately visible right in front of us. Vision does not determine *what* we see with our eyes; vision determines *how* we see with our eyes.

> Why is vision so important in the life of faith? How can people posture themselves in such a way to "see what God is doing"?

> How do you feel about the statement "It is not a question of whether God is doing something but whether we are able to see what God is doing"? Does that ring true for you? Why or why not?

FROM THE BIBLE

Read Joshua 5:13–15 (NIV):

> Now when Joshua was near Jericho, he looked up and saw a man standing in front of him with a drawn sword in his hand. Joshua went up to him and asked, "Are you for us or for our enemies?" "Neither," he replied, "but as commander of the army of the LORD I have now come." Then Joshua fell facedown to the ground in reverence, and asked him, "What message does my Lord have for his servant?" The commander of the LORD's army replied, "Take off your sandals, for the place where you are standing is holy." And Joshua did so.

NEW NORMAL STUDY GUIDE

Joshua was gazing at the fortified city of Jericho protected by its storied walls when he looked up one day to see an ominous sight: a large man standing over him with his sword drawn. He seemed to have come out of nowhere. If we reimagine this as a scene out of an old Western movie, Joshua, the gunslinger, would be the kind of man who lived with his finger on the trigger. Nobody got the drop on him, nobody sneaked up on him, and nobody surprised him until this being did! This angelic visitor was not just any angel; this being was the commander of the Lord's army.

I might have fainted at the sight, but Joshua asked the mysterious stranger a perfectly rational question: "Are you for us or for our enemies?" (Josh. 5:13, NIV). It wasn't a bad question, and in a way maybe it was the only question he could have asked. But it was a very human question—a question based on what he could see with his eyes. Are you on my team or theirs? Are you for me or against me? Are you a friend or a foe?

Because Joshua was a spiritual man, a humble and discerning man, who was asking earnest questions and seeking the truth, he was in a position to hear an astonishing answer: "Neither...but as commander of the army of the LORD I have now come" (v. 14, NIV). And just like that, *snap*! Joshua's perspective completely shifted from a horizontal human perspective to a vertical one, able to see that this was not a mere human encounter at all but a holy visitation.

To this day scholars disagree as to the exact nature of the mysterious stranger who visited Joshua. Was it an angel? Was this an appearance of the preincarnate Christ? Was Joshua the first person to have a conversation with Christ this way? We don't know for certain. But for our purpose, the exact nature of this unusual visitor is not critical.

More pertinent is that Joshua has an alert, clearheaded awareness that comes from abiding in the presence of God. He has been praying and waiting on God. He is on high alert. When you pray, you can count on it—whatever needs to be seen will be seen.

But Joshua's interest is not the same as the angelic being's interest. Joshua wants to know, "Are you for me or against me?" But the stranger has a bigger concern than winning any particular battle that Joshua has in mind. The priority of this incredible being is to serve God and accomplish His purpose.

Because Joshua was prayerful and stayed close to the presence of God, his response was not to try to convince the stranger of his plan or argue his case. Instead, he discerned the larger purpose of God through the presence of this stranger. Once Joshua discerned that this commander had been sent for a higher purpose, his immediate response was to fall to the ground in worship. He was willing to submit his way of seeing to another way of seeing.

Joshua asked, "What does my lord say to his servant?" (v. 14). He was instantly submissive to the will of God, willing to subordinate his desires, his agenda, and his way of seeing things to whatever God had planned for him. No longer was it about winning or losing; conquering Jericho became secondary to doing God's will. More than personal victory, he wanted to honor and worship God, no matter what that meant or what it cost.

> Joshua assumed that the stranger was on either his side or his enemy's side—but the man said he was on "neither" but the Lord's side. Does the world seem as if it mostly still defaults to the same kind of binary, "you are either on my team or their team," thinking? How does that play out, say, on social media?

> Can you think of a time in your own life when you were so focused on winning a particular battle you felt you needed to win that you couldn't see the bigger picture of what God was doing?

BELIEVE FOR CHANGE

> What struggle or conflict in your life have you only been seeing from a natural, or physical, point of view that God might want to show you from a spiritual perspective? Ask the Holy Spirit to show you a situation right now that you are only seeing from a human vantage point that God wants to show you from a divine vantage point. Write down any impressions or thoughts that come to you in the silence.

IN MY LIFE

> What stands out for you from the study this week?

> What adjustments will you make in your life because of what you've learned?

> How will your relationship with God and your relationships with others change?

Session 5

PRAISE PAVES THE WAY

THIS SESSION IS a companion to chapter 7 of *New Normal*.

FOCUS IN

> Have you ever had a moment in your life when you were so overcome with gratitude or thanksgiving—or maybe just with pure, exhilarating joy—that you let yourself go in a primal expression of praise? When you expressed how grateful you were in a way that might have seemed a little bit intense to others?

A PERSONAL WORD

I'll never forget when we were getting ready to build the south campus at James River Church in 1999. We felt as if God was truly calling us to expand our ministry and that a new and larger location to connect with more people in our community would be critical. At the time, we only had a tiny fraction in the bank of what it would take to do it. Y2K was looming large in people's minds then, and that anxiety penetrated the financial sphere. Our resources as a church were earmarked, and I simply could not see how we could take the step of building a new worship center.

It felt as if our plane were on the runway but didn't have the fuel to take off.

I had been invited by Pastor Jim Cymbala to preach at the Brooklyn Tabernacle. That evening we stayed for service, and at the close, Pastor Cymbala invited those with needs to come forward and worship the Lord, believing that act of faith would change their situation. As I spent that time in prayer and worship, I didn't feel anything and I didn't hear the Lord speak anything. As we left the church and headed to the hotel, I still felt both discouraged and overwhelmed.

The next morning when I got up and boarded the flight back to Springfield, as I sat waiting for takeoff, I knew that something in me had shifted. Suddenly I saw the whole thing differently—I saw through the eyes of faith. God had done something in that evening prayer time that restored my vision even though I was unaware of it at the time. I opened my Bible and read Genesis 12, where God promised to give Abraham the land. Having received a promise that doubtless seemed impossible, Abraham built an altar and worshipped there. In that deep interior way, I heard what I believe was the Spirit of God whisper to me, telling me to build an altar of praise on that new property where the new building's platform was going to be.

The next morning, I drove to the land in my pickup, and with the morning rush-hour traffic speeding by on the highway, I lifted my hands in praise and began thanking the Lord, saying, "If You say there's going to be an auditorium here, I believe You, and I will worship You." It was the shout of praise before the battle. It was the shout of faith in the face of impossibility. The shout signifies letting go of ego, letting go of attempts to intellectualize, rationalize, and work it all out, and entering into that simple trust that God will do what He promised. The shout is the move from the rational to the transrational, from giving it my best to trusting God to do what only God can do! And by the time it was all said and done, we were able to build that building, as God provided the funds in ways that I never imagined possible.

You might not be called to build a new church building, but I absolutely believe there is a field of faith, a promise God has given you that on a human plane seems impossible. Only you can build an altar there. Only you can pick the rocks to signify what God has done and what you believe God will do. Only you can sing your song and play your trumpet or your air guitar! No one else can shout for you. No one else can be a substitute for your praise.

God has promised you that you can enter the new normal. He has prepared this place for you. You don't have to make it happen. You just have to shout for it, to praise God as if it has already happened! And the walls that once seemed insurmountable will surely crumble before the power of the living God.

REFLECTION

➤ Have you ever felt drawn to praise God for something before it actually happened? Why do you think it is significant that we are called to worship *before* God acts on our behalf?

➤ What do you think about the whole idea of praising God before the victory comes? Does that feel hopeful? Scary? Too much like it is a way of just clicking your heels together three times and wishing really hard? Or do you feel as if it's possible that giving God praise before anything actually shifts in your life might actually change something?

FROM THE BIBLE

Read Joshua 6:1–16.

It is necessary in a life of faith that you show up at the same time, at the same place, to do the same thing, and sometimes it is necessary to have such times even when nothing visibly happens. We see it when Joshua and the people march around the city day after day and nothing changes. Nothing changes on Sunday. Nothing changes on Monday. Nothing changes on Tuesday. Nothing changes on Wednesday. Nothing changes on Thursday. Nothing changes on Friday. Nothing changes on Saturday either—not after the first march around the city. Nor after the second. Nor after the third, the fourth, the fifth, or the sixth. It can feel long and monotonous when nothing you can see with your eyes is changing yet. Absolutely nothing you can see is changing—*until everything does.*

But it is also necessary to have time and space set aside for something wilder, less predictable, and more spontaneous—there has to be time and space set aside *for the shout* because ultimately God did not use swords to bring His people the victory. He did not use battering rams or rely on the strategy of expert military tacticians. No, the primary weapon God used was *praise*—and the sharpest point of that weapon was the *shout*! After the monotony and routine, God *commanded* them to shout, to let go, to let everything inside them out, to move from the practice of routine obedience to the release of faith-filled praise: "When you hear them sound a long blast on the trumpets, have the whole army give a loud shout; then the wall of the city will collapse and the army will go up, everyone straight in" (Josh. 6:5, NIV).

You can't have one without the other—the shout without the routine, or the routine without the shout.

Both are equally important parts of the journey into a new land. Both are needed. But it is when they enter the complete abandon of the shout that the walls finally crumble! The shattering of the walls is up to God. The shout is up to us!

And while the walk around the walls before may have been uneventful, the shout is anything but. According to Joshua 6:5 (NIV), the shout was loud. God told Joshua to "have the whole army give a loud shout." Again, in verse 20, we read that "the men gave a loud shout" (NIV). Volume matters to God!

The shout is not an optional part of life with God; the shout is essential. If you are to enter the new normal God has for you, your shouts of praise will have to get louder than the battle you are facing!

And what kind of shout is this? We know this much: the shout was celebratory. The Jews used two types of trumpets: those made of silver and those made of rams' horns. The common Hebrew word for trumpet is *shofar*; for ram's horn, it is *jobel*, which is the root of the word *Jubilee*. The priests used the silver trumpets to signal the camp when something important was happening (as in Numbers 10). Rams' horns, however, were used primarily for celebrations!

The priests didn't use the silver trumpets as they finished their march around Jericho, because Israel wasn't declaring war on Jericho—for there was no war. They weren't declaring war but declaring victory! There is power in thanking God in advance of the victory. There is power in praising God before we have seen anything change. There's power in audibly, vocally celebrating what God will do. It actively builds your confidence and strengthens your faith that He is going to do it!

The sequence of the shout is equally important—the shout came *before* the victory. Joshua 6:5, again, says, "When you hear them sound a long blast on the trumpets, have the whole army give a loud shout; *then the wall of the city will collapse*" (NIV, emphasis added). And Joshua 6:20 says, "So the people shouted when the priests blew the trumpets. And it happened when the people heard the sound of the trumpet, and the people shouted with a great shout, that the wall fell down flat. *Then* the people went up into the city" (NKJV, emphasis added). The shout came before—not after—the walls came down!

> ➤ Do you come from a faith tradition where shouting, celebration, dancing, open expressions of joy, and so on are common and acceptable, or where they are frowned upon? When you hear the language of "a shout," what emotion does that stir in you? Does that sound like freedom and joy to you? Or does that language scare you a little?

> What language or expression of praise comes the most naturally for you?

> Some people may feel more comfortable than others expressing outward emotions. What do you think—is whether you find your "shout" merely about whether you are an introvert or an extrovert? Do quiet, introverted, more emotionally reserved people still find a way to "shout"?

> Do you believe that routine ("liturgy"— showing up at the same time at the same place doing the same thing) and acts of spontaneity and exuberance are both necessary in the life of faith? Do you think one is more important than the other, or are they equally necessary in a journey of spiritual growth and transformation?

BELIEVE FOR CHANGE

The best way to learn about praise is to, well, praise! That's what is so wonderful about it—you don't have to attend seminars or go to classes first, or learn a formula or a program or a doctrine of praise. You don't have the answer yet, the solution, the victory, or anything in your life worked out yet. We praise what we love, and when we praise from the depths of us, whatever form it takes, it will be beautiful to God. What praise does take, as we see in this story, is set-aside time and space.

> ➤ Just before you set aside time and space to praise, take a few moments just to remember the One you are praising and all the reasons you have to praise Him. Make two lists: one of things you adore about God and one of things in your life you have to be grateful for.

> ➤ Set aside time and space for intentional praise—preferably like what we read in Joshua, space for your "shout"—for you to praise in whatever way feels the most primal, authentic, and from the depths for you. If you can get lost the most in the presence of God on a hike, then set aside time to adore God

on a hike. If you can get lost the most in the worship of God with a particular song turned up loud in your car, where you can sing along as loud as you want without feeling self-conscious, plan a drive. The key is simply to make it an intentional, designated time with no other agenda except to praise!

> If you are doing this study as a group, you might consider incorporating a time of intentional praise together. Maybe somebody in your group plays a guitar or other instrument. Or you could try singing a hymn or worship song a cappella together. It could be awkward, but it also could be incredibly powerful or really fun—or quite possibly all of the above!

IN MY LIFE

> What stands out for you from the study this week?

➤ What adjustments will you make in your life because of what you've learned?

➤ How will your relationship with God and your relationships with others change?

Session 6

THE LAW OF FIRST THINGS

THIS SESSION IS a companion to chapter 8 of *New Normal.*

FOCUS IN

> It's sometimes considered taboo to talk about the relationship between our faith and our money, or our faith and our stuff. How about for you? Does it make you uncomfortable when people talk about money/possessions in church and/or faith spaces? Do you think it is important to discuss these topics within our faith communities, or do you think of them as private matters?

A PERSONAL WORD

Before I tell you what the law of first things means, let me tell you what it doesn't mean: it does not mean God is a greedy cosmic version of the godfather, threatening to shake you down if He doesn't get His cut in time. Jesus is not standing in front of you, holding an offering plate and saying in an Italian accent, "I'm gonna make you an offer you can't refuse." The law of first things is not about threats or retaliation. It's about reciprocity. Everything in the kingdom of God requires reciprocity: we freely receive; we freely give. Both actions require open hands. No wonder it's required that we honor God first; it's precisely in the act of giving that we open ourselves up to receive God's provision.

What we do with the first part determines what happens with the rest. This principle is embedded in the narrative of Scripture over and over again. Exodus 34:20 says, "The firstborn of a donkey you shall redeem with a lamb, or if you will not redeem it you shall break its neck." It may sound like a cryptic, violent image, but the idea is that you would be better off not having the animal at all than keeping what is God's, because if you keep it—if you live from a posture of clinging, holding on, being stingy, being miserly, or having fear and control—everything is cursed. On the other hand, when you give back to God—living from a place of release, freedom, and trust—everything is blessed!

God reinforces this promise repeatedly to His people. In Proverbs 3:9–10, He says, "Honor the LORD with your wealth and with the firstfruits of all your produce; then your barns will be filled with plenty, and your vats will be bursting with wine." It was the very founding promise God made to Israel's ancestor Abraham: "Because you have done this and have not withheld your son, your only son, I will surely bless you, and I will surely multiply your offspring as the stars of heaven and as the sand that is on the sea-shore" (Gen. 22:16–17). This promise was so great, so sweeping in scope, that because Abraham did not withhold what was most dear to him, God promised that through him and his lineage, all the families of the earth would be blessed (v. 18).

I just want to offer this by way of testimony—this is not empty preacher talk for me. This principle, this law of first things, is *true, true, true*. It's the kind of truth I feel in my bones. I feel urgent about it—not because I have something to gain from any of this but because I've seen the truth of it play out consistently throughout my life. I grew up on a farm in eastern Colorado, where three generations of Lindells made their living by sowing and reaping; therefore, none of this is abstract to me. The law of first things, which farmers would recognize as the law of the harvest, is *very* real to me. I know that if you plant one kernel of corn, you get three ears of corn, and that three ears of corn will have a minimum of six hundred kernels per ear. A farmer can literally calculate their harvest based on how much seed they plant.

So how does this principle translate to our lives? It doesn't mean everybody will drive a Ferrari, but it does mean there will be provision. Even people who are not Christians recognize something of the truth of this. From the language around the law of attraction to new age and self-help business gurus, anybody paying attention to how the world works has to acknowledge that a person reaps what they sow. It almost seems counterintuitive, but those who clench their fists lose what they have; those who open their hands are able to be given more.

As I look back over my life, again and again, I have watched the Lord multiply whatever I have placed in His hands. And I am not alone in learning this principle is true. Saints throughout the ages have understood the law of the harvest. John Bunyan, the author of the Christian classic *The Pilgrim's Progress*, wrote, "A man there was, and they called him mad; the more he gave, the more he had."[1] God can only bless what we give Him.

REFLECTION

> How is the law of first things different from giving to get?

> Do you think there are people who stumble into the truth of the law of first things who may not even share your faith or belief system? Does it only apply to people who have been formally taught it or understand it within the church, or do you think the law of first things operates more like a universal principle that is true for all people in all places, no matter where they come from?

> Why do you think it is that those who clench
  their fists tend to lose what they have, while
  those who open their hands are given more?
  Why is it impossible to receive God's goodness and provision when you have clenched
  fists?

What we do or don't do with what God has placed
in our hands has a real and lasting effect on the people
around us; it can either bring blessing and abundance or a curse. The way of openness, sharing, and
reciprocity is the way of the King and the way of the
kingdom. If we live with open hands and open hearts,
we will be blessed and open up a way of blessing for
the people around us. But if we live miserly, grasping,
conserving lives, only concerned about meeting the
immediate needs of me and mine, that selfishness
cuts off the flow of divine blessing to the people
around us too. For modern people living in Western
cultures, the idea that we are somehow responsible
for one another or that our lives are somehow bound
together can seem strange. But ancient peoples and
more Eastern cultures have always understood that
none of us live in a vacuum.

> Can you think of a time in your life when you may have unintentionally squandered what God had given you in terms of time, talents, and resources in the name of paying bills or meeting your own needs?

FROM THE BIBLE

Read Joshua 6:16–19 and 7:1–26, especially noting 6:19: "But all silver and gold, and every vessel of bronze and iron, are holy to the LORD; they shall go into the treasury of the LORD."

When the Israelites took Jericho, they were given explicit instructions: only Rahab (the prostitute who had hidden two of their spies) and those with her were to be spared. They were also given instruction not to take any of the articles of silver, gold, bronze, and iron, which along with expensive items of clothing, were to be consecrated to the Lord and placed in the Lord's treasury (Josh. 6:16–19).

One man, Achan, decided not to comply. He was not an evil man, per se. I imagine that, like us, he was a man with bills to pay. And after such a massive victory for the entire nation, he probably figured nobody would be all that bothered if he kept just a couple of things for himself. He didn't take all the exotic treasure—just some of it, just a cloak, a few pieces of silver, and a bar of gold. It wasn't enough for anybody else to notice. It was petty theft at best. It certainly wasn't murder, in any case. At first, it reads as if it might not be more than a footnote to the story.

Later on, when his folly is exposed, it becomes clearer that Achan keeping these things was important enough to interfere with the favor and blessing of God resting on an entire people. But before you start booing and hissing at Achan, keep in mind that he had legitimate needs that motivated him, just as you do.

We have no idea what kind of hardship brought him into this moment. We can presume that this entire journey of coming into the land had been hard for all God's people. Don't be too quick to villainize Achan, or you won't realize how quickly you can become him. He was a guy who put his own needs above the needs of others. That's what this entire story illustrates: selfishness, greed, and holding back instead of giving back will stop the flow of God's blessing.

In shorthand, we might even say it like this: Achan was a pragmatist. When Jericho was full of expensive treasure and even a little of that treasure would go a long way in paying some bills, taking some of that treasure made all the sense in the world, practically speaking. That's the trouble with thinking pragmatically. You can always justify holding on to the money. You can always justify why you need the money more than God does, more than the poor do.

You can always come up with a perfectly good reason the rule doesn't apply to you. Once again, this isn't some kind of over-the-top, overt evil. It is where limited, human-scarcity thinking gets you, instead of the kind of abundance thinking that God calls for, which would open both your hands and heart.

As the story continues, we discover that Achan's disobedience was indeed more than a footnote. God was greatly displeased because of it. Jericho had been conquered, and next on the horizon was the city of Ai. Joshua decided to send only three thousand men to Ai after some of his scouts reported seeing only a few people there. Jericho had seemed impossible at first, but God had given them the victory. Ai looked as if it would be a cakewalk. Instead, the army of Israel was routed, a disastrous defeat. Thirty-six Israelite warriors were cut down, and the rest of them were chased out of town. After the elation and jubilation of their soaring win at Jericho, the defeat completely took the life out of them. The words of the text are haunting: "And the hearts of the people melted and became as water" (Josh. 7:5).

In response to this, Joshua tore his clothes and fell facedown before God until evening. It was then that God told him Israel sinned against Him by taking the devoted things and were therefore defeated. Victory would be impossible until the people of Israel gave the Lord what belonged to Him.

The image is a stark, poignant one. Again, the law of first things shows us that the first part of all God gives us should be given back to Him and that what we do with the first part determines what happens to the rest. Perhaps there was a time when you or I did not know this. But once we come to see the truth of it, we have a consequential decision to make. We must acknowledge the very real truth that as long as we think we possess things our possessions possess us. We do not own; we only steward. God freely gives to us, and He calls us to give back to Him freely. When we live as people who believe it all belongs to God, we live immersed in reality, and it opens up the door for every good gift.

We ignore this principle at our peril. God's principles are not arbitrary. This principle matters because our generosity with God determines whether we will be generous with others. It determines what kind of people we will be in the world and what kind of world we will make—whether we will be closefisted people or openhanded people.

When the topic of generosity comes up, it's easy to be defensive and insist that we are only trying to look out for our needs. But a theology of scarcity (as opposed to abundance) is closely related to a theology of selfishness. And when we put ourselves first, all kinds of bad things happen. We can justify anything when we rationalize putting our needs above those of others. It's where most evil in the world begins—not with malicious intent but with people simply placing their needs above the needs of their community.

› What are some of the reasons we might find
ourselves unintentionally justifying putting
our own needs over the needs of the community? What might some of the unintended
consequences be?

› How did the story of Achan make you feel as
you read it? Choose from this list of words the
one you would use to best describe the story,
and then take a few moments to write down
why that word is most descriptive for you:

» Sobering

» Disturbing

» Provocative

» Harsh

» Challenging

» Motivating

» Instructive

» Just/fair

> ➤ Has there ever been a time in your life when you were dishonest because you were afraid there wasn't going to be enough for you, when you took something you shouldn't have or kept something you shouldn't have because you were driven by the fear of scarcity?

> ➤ Would Achan's sin ever have existed in a community where everyone genuinely believed that there *would always be enough*? How does whether we believe we have a god of scarcity or a God of abundance make a difference in how we behave in our lives?

BELIEVE FOR CHANGE

> ➤ What would it mean for you to live as if you really did believe that what you do with your stuff actually does matter to God and to others? How would you live differently? Achan tried to keep the treasures back for himself and never got a chance to make it right—but we do get that chance. Take a few moments

to pray and ask God to show you any ways that you might currently be putting your own needs above what God is asking you to do and above the needs of the people around you. Write three to five of those things down, whatever comes to your mind. What would it look like to repent, to have a change of mind, to actually begin to live as if you believe/think differently?

IN MY LIFE

› What stands out for you from the study this week?

› What adjustments will you make in your life because of what you've learned?

> How will your relationship with God and
> your relationships with others change?

Session 7

ASKING FOR DIRECTIONS

THIS SESSION IS a companion to chapters 9 and 10 of *New Normal*.

FOCUS IN

> Have you ever had the experience of being lost before and still somehow not being able or willing to find it in yourself to ask for directions? If so, that seems to be a pretty standard issue in human experience. Why do you think that is? What is it that gets in the way of us asking for directions (ahem—OK, perhaps especially those of us who are *men*!), even when we know we need help?

A PERSONAL WORD

We do not need to live in fear, panic, paranoia, or insecurity. We do, on the other hand, need to ask God about *everything*. We should never assume we know the answer. Presumption is our worst enemy. At James River we have made prayer our central focus because we are convinced that prayer is crucial. We aren't more spiritual, wiser, or better than anyone else. We just aim to be more dependent!

The Book of James says, "You do not have, because you do not ask" (4:2). God is eager to give us counsel, guidance, and direction. He is a communicative God who is always speaking, but we are often slow to listen.

Prayer is the key to *everything* in a life with God and beyond! If we pray, God *is* going to show us what to do. No experience, special training, or education is required, only a free and honest admission that we don't know what's next and we need God to show us. Extra-special holiness isn't asked of us; humility is. If we are willing to take the time to ask, God is always willing to answer. Directions aren't for those who are smart, just for those who are looking.

Often we are just too smart for our good. In our endless desire for knowledge and understanding, and now our seemingly endless access to information— podcasts, articles, and a plethora of online content— we outsmart ourselves. Wisdom begins when we get to the end of ourselves and realize our understanding, however well-informed, is never enough and that our deep need is to trust in something beyond ourselves. We live in a time in which we have unprecedented access to information at our fingertips. Yet it is not more information that we need but more trust. We don't need more self-dependence; we need to become more at home in our native dependence.

Our default, all too often, is to think we know the answers or at least to think we ought to know them. But we were meant to rely on something and someone greater than ourselves, made not just to know but to ask, to wonder, and to trust. What would it look like to stop trying to stockpile information, or even to live as if you are supposed to know the truth somehow? What would it look like to ask for directions, to admit to the limitations of our very human, often superficial way of seeing and judging on appearances and instead rely on the Spirit, who knows and searches the depths of our hearts and reveals the very heart of God to us?

Even the best of us are prone to deception—especially deceiving ourselves, as unreflective and unaware as we often are of our motives. That's why *discernment* is such a vital word for Christians, prayerfully relying on the wisdom of the Holy Spirit to show us what we would never see in our one-dimensional way of viewing the world. There is so much we simply do not know that only God can show us. And God does not show us unless we have the humility to ask!

REFLECTION

> Do you find it easier to seek out information or research a thing than to pray about it? Does it feel more natural to try and figure it out on your own or ask someone else than to ask God what to do? If so, why do you think that is?

> Have you ever asked God to guide or direct you in something when you were at a significant crossroads in your life and felt as if God responded in a clear way? If so, what was that experience, and what did you learn from it?

> Does God speak to some people more than others, or is it just that some of us are more attentive to God than others, that some of us are more intentional about listening?

> Are there particular questions that have been tugging at your mind and heart, things that have been coming up when you lay your head on the pillow or when you are in the shower? Something that is worrying you but may not yet have even crossed your mind to inquire of the Lord about? Maybe a need for direction or guidance that actually seemed *too small* to ask about? If it concerns you, it concerns God, who is mindful of every detail of your life, who has numbered every hair on your head. Instead of worrying about it another moment,

having it stuck in your head, why not just ask God about it right now? Instead of speculating, wondering, or theorizing, why not just ask and give God a chance to respond? And as a way of getting whatever question weighs on you out of your mind and handing it over, why not go ahead and write down a couple of the questions that are most pressing on you right now?

We are supposed to talk to God freely, all the time about everything. But there is not only a place and time to ask for wisdom and direction but also a time to make crazy-big requests. As I mentioned earlier, every August our church does twenty-one days of fasting and prayer because we know that some things will not happen unless we fast and pray. The theme for our fast in 2020 was "Mountains Will Move." In the middle of the fast I was diagnosed with prostate cancer. It didn't catch me by surprise because my PSA level had been gradually increasing. For those not familiar with the term PSA, the letters don't stand for "public service announcement" but for "prostate-specific antigen." It is one means of discerning if a man has prostate cancer. With my PSA number gradually increasing, my doctor had suggested a biopsy, and the results came back positive for cancer. Because the church was fasting and praying, I knew I wanted them to join me in praying for the mountain of cancer to move, and I believed God was going to do something supernatural in response to our prayers.

As we made the announcement asking them to pray, an interesting thing happened. I couldn't stop smiling! I felt a joy in my heart like I had never felt before. The Lord opened the door for me to participate in a clinical trial that involved a new approach to treating prostate cancer. Within two weeks of having my biopsy, I was cancer-free and back preaching at James River Church. The Lord had moved the mountain, but even more, during those two weeks, both Debbie and I experienced a joy we had never known in our entire lives. It was a reminder that God can move mountains, but He does even more than move mountains! If mountains need to be moved in your life, remember there is a God who delights in doing the impossible—and even more!

> Have you ever had to make a crazy-big request of your own? Have you ever had God answer one?

NEW NORMAL STUDY GUIDE

> What, if anything, might hold you back from
  making a crazy-big request now?

FROM THE BIBLE

Within just two verses a chapter apart in Joshua, we
get two radically different approaches to prayer—and
to life, for that matter. Joshua 9:14 says, "The Israelites
sampled their provisions but did not inquire of the
LORD" (NIV). There is no dramatic sin or horrible evil
act—the leaders of God's people simply fail to ask
God for directions, resulting in all sorts of unnecessary confusion that will have implications for generations to come (as seen in chapter 9 of *New Normal*).

But in Joshua 10:14 we read a very different report:
"There has never been a day like it before or since, a
day when the LORD listened to a human being. Surely
the LORD was fighting for Israel!" (NIV). Whereas in
one story we see the people seemingly just forget to
consult with God before making a decision and all
the mischief that comes in the wake of their failure
to pray, we see just how far God is willing to go in
order to respond to the cries of God's people a chapter
later—when God's response to the prayer of Joshua
is actually to *make the sun stand still*! It is truly an
extraordinary event never again to be duplicated in
Scripture. "Joshua spoke to the LORD...and he said

in the sight of Israel, 'Sun, stand still at Gibeon, and moon, in the Valley of Aijalon.' And the sun stood still, and the moon stopped, until the nation took vengeance on their enemies" (vv. 12–13).

It boggles the mind to imagine a scene in which the laws of science are suspended in response to one man's prayer. "There has been no day like it before or since, when the LORD heeded the voice of a man, for the LORD fought for Israel" (v. 14). Even this description carries a trace of understatement. How could there ever be such a day to compare to this?

When he was Moses' lowly assistant, Joshua could have scarcely imagined leading his people over the Jordan River. Yet by this point in the story, he was so fully convinced of the goodness and faithfulness of God that he made a request so audacious it seemed almost comical: he requested that the sun stand still, that the stars and elements themselves would bend to the power of the living God.

This was not arrogance or hubris—this was the natural expression of a man growing accustomed to seeing God bend the rules of possibility. His faith was slowly becoming larger, more spacious, and more audacious to make room for the vastness of his God. Joshua had seen God do it too many times. He knew now that nothing was impossible for God, and he spoke and acted from that place of deep conviction. Not only did the sun stand still, but all five kings were defeated. By way of epilogue the Book of Joshua records, "So Joshua took the whole land," and then beautifully adds, "And the land had rest from war" (11:23).

What do we make of such exploits? Gradually throughout the Book of Joshua we see his faith (and the faith of his people) grow, until ultimately there was nothing he would not ask and nothing he would not believe his God could do! When a person comes to know and trust God in this way, nothing is impossible and nothing is unimaginable. There are no limits to a life lived from this kind of deep, abiding trust.

> What is the thing in your life, or in the life of someone you love right now, that would require nothing less than this kind of direct divine intervention? What would require a straight-up, sun-stand-still kind of miracle? What is the thing you desperately want God to do but are afraid to ask because it seems too big or you don't feel worthy enough? What is your one crazy-big request? Write it down.

BELIEVE FOR CHANGE

> Remember just how much God delights in giving good things to His kids! Jesus Himself taught us this. Take a few minutes to read

these words slowly, preferably three or four times, meditating on them. Let them wash over you and get onto you and into you: "Ask and it will be given to you; seek and you will find; knock and the door will be opened to you. For everyone who asks receives; the one who seeks finds; and to the one who knocks, the door will be opened. Which of you, if your son asks for bread, will give him a stone? Or if he asks for a fish, will give him a snake? If you, then, though you are evil, know how to give good gifts to your children, how much more will your Father in heaven give good gifts to those who ask him!" (Matt. 7:7–11, NIV). Pause to breathe in those words for just a moment. Let them fill you up. Can you *feel* the truth of them? God loves to give His children good gifts; He is on pins and needles just waiting for you to *ask*. Nothing, absolutely nothing, you will ever ask is too difficult for God to do, and there are no lengths He is unwilling to go to, to demonstrate the depths of His love for you.

➤ Since God has been waiting for you to ask, don't put it off any longer. *Ask.* Unload all of it, every care, every concern. Pour all of it out. If you are doing the study as a group, consider allowing each person (if, and only if, they feel comfortable) time to share their crazy-big request, and take time as a group to pray specifically for one another.

IN MY LIFE

> What stands out for you from the study this week?

> What adjustments will you make in your life because of what you've learned?

> How will your relationship with God and your relationships with others change?

Session 8

LIVING FOR LEGACY

T
THIS SESSION IS a companion to chapters 10 and 11 of *New Normal*.

FOCUS IN

> Who is someone in your life who has left a legacy that has marked you? What is it about that person that impacted you so much?

A PERSONAL WORD

Years later, both in the words of the aging Joshua and the wrinkles of his weathered old friend Caleb, we see a legacy being shaped that will affect the story of God and of God's people throughout history. On this end of a long history, it's easy to think that these heroes were somehow fundamentally different from us, or that they lived in a world that had no semblance to ours. But the truth is that while Joshua and Caleb were heroes of the faith, they were *not superheroes*. They had no special powers.

What Joshua 14:14 does tell us about the legacy of Caleb is that "Hebron has belonged to Caleb son of Jephunneh the Kenizzite ever since, because he followed the LORD, the God of Israel, wholeheartedly" (NIV). In the vernacular of teenagers in the last few years, Caleb was *extra*. He was full-on. While God has never been looking for people with extra talent, ability, charisma, or resources, when it comes to heart, God is always looking for *extra*. God loves big, wholehearted, full-on devotion. God loves it when people hold nothing back and give without reserve of their whole, deepest, truest selves.

We talk a lot in church circles about wanting more of God, but truthfully, all of God is always accessible to God's sons and daughters. We can have as much of God—His presence and goodness—as we want. That is never in question. God loves to give good gifts to His children! The issue is not us getting more of God but *God getting more of us.* Are we willing to let go of every inhibition that has held us back before? Are we willing to be completely devoted, free from every hesitation? Are we willing to be *uninhibited*?

When the Book of Joshua introduces Caleb, being wholehearted is the one thing he is known for. It is the characteristic for which the ancient Hebrew tradition will forever remember him. Scripture says the same thing about him every time: he followed the Lord *wholeheartedly*. Numbers 14:24 frames it this way: "But because my servant Caleb *has a different spirit and follows me wholeheartedly,* I will bring him into the land he went to, and his descendants will inherit it" (NIV, emphasis added).

We live in a time in which nearly everyone in our culture is obsessed with being different, finding their niche, and figuring out what will make them stand out. It doesn't matter if you're in middle school or middle management, on social media or socializing at a party—everybody wants to find what sets them apart. Whether it's a haircut, a quirky car, a foreign film collection, a college football team, or a genre of music, there are countless things we can find to define us as different. Of course, there is nothing inherently wrong with self-expression, but the relentless pursuit of it as a tool to define us can be nothing less than exhausting. The pursuit of self-expression becomes relentless precisely because we look to external things to tell us (and others) who we are.

Not so with God! As Scripture tells us, "Man looks on the outward appearance, but the LORD looks on the heart" (1 Sam. 16:7). God isn't interested in hairstyles or hobbies; God is interested in your heart. God doesn't need more stuff; God needs more *you*. God wants more of what is inside. It is your heart that fascinates Him. He longs for what's inside you. So many people in your life make you feel as if you need to be smarter, savvier, more beautiful, more this, or more that. God doesn't want anything in this world—except *more of you*.

REFLECTION

> ‣ Do you ever think about your legacy? What would you want it to be, among your friends, family, the people whom you love and who love you the most? Take a few moments to simply make a list of words—not sentences—you

would want to be associated with your legacy. What words would you hope would be used to sum up your life, your story, and what it meant to others?

> How might thinking about your legacy (in the future) change the way you live your life right now (in the present)?

> How might people who believe in and follow the God of Joshua think differently from those who do not attempt to follow God about what does and does not matter in a legacy?

If you don't come into the new normal, it won't be because you don't have the natural gifts or ability. It won't be because you weren't the best or brightest. It won't be about natural selection or survival of the fittest. It won't even be because you weren't tough enough. It will be because you weren't willing to pay the price of total commitment. Unfulfilled dreams and unsatiated desires will always characterize a life of halfhearted commitment.

Desire, contrary to popular opinion, is not a dirty word. God longs to "give you the desires of your heart" (Ps. 37:4). But for our desires to be trusted, we have to commit our hearts to God first. Doing this creates boundaries for our desires, causing us to desire what is best for us and what God desires for us. When we commit ourselves fully to God, we will want what God wants for us because we trust that what God wants is always good.

After all, God desires that we would possess the land—not a part or piece of the land but all of it. God wants us to be spiritually, emotionally, and psychologically whole. God wants to bring us into the new normal where our relationships are at peace and we have favor in our work. Everywhere we go, everywhere our feet touch, we bring the grace of God with us. The rule and reign of heaven come to earth until that prayer is finally fulfilled that the followers of Jesus have been praying for two thousand years: "Your kingdom come, your will be done, on earth as it is in heaven" (Matt. 6:10).

> If living this kind of life requires being *whole-hearted*, that means it has to be fully chosen. That doesn't mean you have to feel like doing everything that you are doing all the time, but

you do, on some level, have to want this kind of life—or at least want to want it! So here's a loaded question: *What do you want?* I do not mean superficial, top-level wants—what do you *really*, truly want in your deepest self? Make a list of some of the things you actually, deeply desire.

> Is *desire* a good or bad word where you come from? How might it change your life to come to truly believe that God *actually does* want to give you the desires of your heart?

FROM THE BIBLE

Like the old man Caleb, Joshua lived to see God do extraordinary things in his life and the lives of the people he loved. He occupied the land and saw the walls of Jericho fall. He saw God do the impossible over and over again. But Joshua's story, like all great stories, would ultimately come to an end. So as he prepared to trust the same God to cross over one more river—not the Jordan this time but the one from this world into the next—he reflected on his life and legacy. Seasoned now from the years of struggle, he gathered the tribes of Israel for one last charge. In a remarkable final address he distilled the wisdom of an undomesticated life full of conquest and battles down to a simple, clear, final challenge. And in short he threw down the gauntlet.

> Now therefore fear the LORD and serve him in sincerity and in faithfulness. Put away the gods that your fathers served beyond the River and in Egypt, and serve the LORD. And if it is evil in your eyes to serve the LORD, choose this day whom you will serve, whether the gods your fathers served in the region beyond the River, or the gods of the Amorites in whose land you dwell. *But as for me and my house, we will serve the LORD.*
>
> —JOSHUA 24:14–15, EMPHASIS ADDED

If Caleb's rousing account of God's faithfulness in his advanced years felt like a kind of rallying cry, Joshua's charge, while no less inspiring, nonetheless leaves us both a challenge and a cautionary note. Joshua and Caleb's generation lived to see the faithfulness of God, and they assure us that God will continue to fulfill His promises and honor His word. But we don't choose to serve God in a vacuum. To serve the God of Abraham, Isaac, and Jacob always puts us in immediate conflict with other gods, with other "principalities" and "powers," in the language of the apostle Paul. (See Ephesians 6:12, NKJV.) We cannot serve God and serve the lesser gods that compete for our love and loyalty. We will have to make a decision.

You will have to make a decision; no one else can make it for you.

Like Caleb's stirring testimony, you can feel the fire coming off these ancient words of Joshua even now, feel the heat and the passion in them. That simple, humble, confessional-but-powerful declaration of Joshua's choice—the choice he made as a young man and reaffirmed every day of his life—was the same choice he actively chose all over again knowing his life was nearly over. Joshua was saying, "I don't know what *y'all* are going to do, but I'm going to tell you right now what my family and I are going to do: we are going to serve the Lord!"

On one level, every generation will have moments to take responsibility for their story. Everybody comes to the moment when they must decide if they will take their place in the ongoing story of God and His people and enter the new normal. But Joshua wisely understood that his story was part of a broader story, a story of a people. His story had real implications for the real lives of people around him—his family, friends, and community. And there is a very real way in which men and women of God have to acknowledge how deeply connected our lives are and, yes, take responsibility for the stories of others. We cannot ultimately control the choices of the people around us. But whether we choose to live faithfully will profoundly affect the shape and character of their journeys.

> While we know how we choose to be in the world with God and others will affect the people around us, we know we do not *control* anyone in our lives, even in our families. The father of the prodigal son in Jesus' famous parable of Luke 15, for example, is a God figure in the story, who also grants his sons freedom to make their own choices. So if we can't exactly *decide* for others, what does it mean to say "as for me and my house, we will serve the Lord"?

> Think about someone who left a legacy in your life that has been mostly positive, faithful, encouraging, or beautiful, and think about someone else who has left a legacy in your life that has been largely full of negativity, harm, or pain. Without making judgments about their character, what differences can you see in the way those two people approached life? How might those differences be instructive in thinking about the kind of legacy you would want to leave?

BELIEVE FOR CHANGE

A lot of people will glimpse the land, the new normal, like a tourist. Many will fly over. Some will even occasionally visit. The land will haunt their dreams. They will almost taste the milk and honey from their pillows, almost feel the lush vegetation of this exotic place from the safety of their beds. And yet most people will only view the land from a distance. They will see God working in someone else's life and imagine it as their own. But they still won't ever come to live this life of radical trust and obedience, come to know the joy and risk of actually *living* in the land.

But as long as you are still breathing, God is still writing your life story. You can live in the land. You can still choose to live and love wholeheartedly, be full-on. You can establish a legacy. In order to live this kind of life, though, we will have to be intentional.

> ➤ In light of everything you have experienced through this study, what are your intentions now? What are your desires? What kind of life do you want from here? How do you see your life and your faith journey differently now than you did when we started?

➤ If someone were to read the story of your life fifty years from now—your legacy, in a single paragraph (not just key words this time)— what would you *want* it to be? Try writing it down.

➤ Especially when we are talking about words such as *legacy* and deciding what kind of people we want to be and how we want the stories of our lives to be told, our written words can be very powerful. Like the stones we read about in Joshua, they too can be altars we can return to, to remember how God spoke to us and moved in us. With that in mind, take a few minutes to write a final prayer that sums up everything stirred up in your heart now as this study comes to a close. Whatever you want to say to God by way of giving thanks, or whatever you would want to ask God to do as a way of sealing this time, let this be a way of building a bridge from this study into the future!

IN MY LIFE

> ➤ What stands out for you from the study this week?

> ➤ What adjustments will you make in your life because of what you've learned?

> ➤ How will your relationship with God and your relationships with others change?

NOTES

SESSION 3

1. Blue Letter Bible, s.v. *"Gilgal,"* accessed January 21, 2021, https://www. blueletterbible.org/lang/Lexicon/Lexicon. cfm?strongs=H1537&t=KJV.

SESSION 6

1. Tryon Edwards, *A Dictionary of Thoughts* (Detroit: F. B. Dickerson Company, 1902), 191, https://www.google.com/books/ edition/A_Dictionary_of_Thoughts/2GxBA QAAMAAJ?hl=en&gbpv=1.